SNOW
LEOPARDS

Contents

Written by Jen Green

Collins

Ghost cat

Snow leopards have pale fur with dark spots. They blend in with the rocks and snow so that they're almost invisible. This natural disguise is called camouflage. In the wild places where snow leopards live, there aren't many people. When they sense humans are close by, snow leopards avoid them. Very few people have ever seen snow leopards in the wild. This is why they're sometimes called ghost cats.

What are snow leopards?

Snow leopards belong to the cat family. This family includes lions, cheetahs and jaguars, as well as pet cats. The cat family is divided into big cats such as lions and tigers, and small cats such as wildcats. Snow leopards are big cats, but they're not as large as lions or tigers.

average height

up to 1 metre

up to 0.5 metres

pet cats
up to 0.75 metres

snow leopards
up to 1.5 metres

tigers
up to 3.5 metres

average length including tail

Leopards are cats with spotted coats. There are three types of leopard: true leopards, snow leopards and clouded leopards. True leopards are close cousins of snow leopards. They live in Africa and southern Asia, where they hunt deer and antelope. They're very good climbers and spend a lot of time in trees. Clouded leopards live in Southeast Asia. They're smaller but also have spotty markings. Snow leopards look a lot like true leopards but live high in the mountains of Central Asia, where it is much colder.

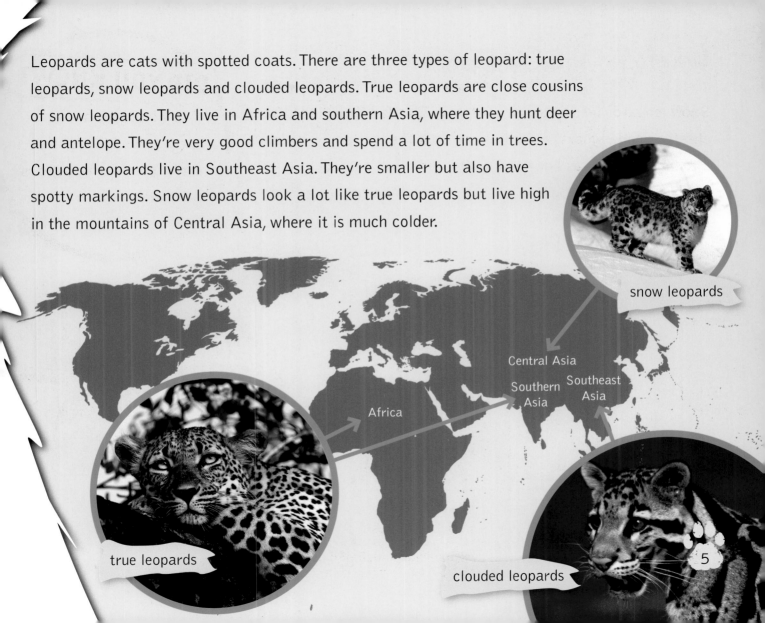

snow leopards

Central Asia

Southern Asia

Southeast Asia

Africa

true leopards

clouded leopards

5

Where do snow leopards live?

Snow leopards are found in many different countries, including India, China, Russia and Mongolia.

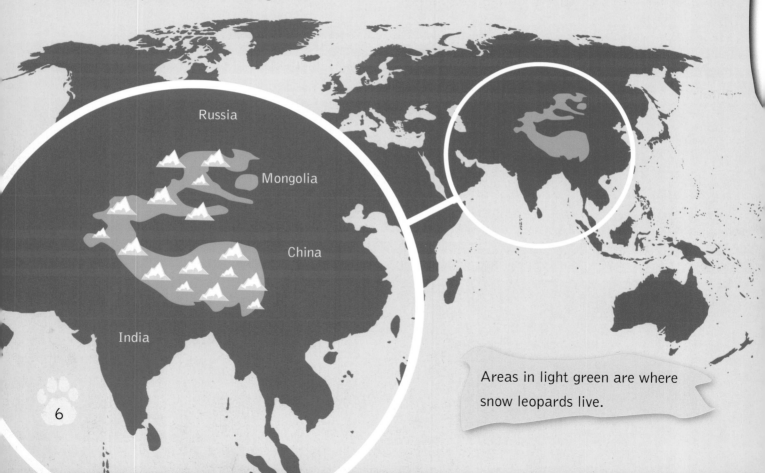

Russia

Mongolia

China

India

Areas in light green are where snow leopards live.

In summer, snow leopards move up the mountains to hunt sheep and goats in the high meadows. When snow falls in autumn, the sheep and goats move down the mountains. They spend winter in forests and valleys because it's warmer there. Snow leopards follow them and take the animals they kill back to their mountain homes.

Most of the time snow leopards hunt on steep hillsides. The rocks are often icy or slippery after rain. Snow leopards' paws have rubbery soles, which grip rock and ice. They can perch on a narrow ledge or chase a goat down a sheer cliff.

Snow cat

In the mountains where snow
leopards live, winters are long
and bitterly cold. At night,
the temperature drops well
below freezing and snow covers
the ground for many months.
Snow leopards' furry coats
grow extra-thick in winter,
which keeps them warm.

Snow leopards' broad, furry
paws act like snowshoes.
They spread the leopards'
weight over a large area,
so they do not sink into soft,
deep snow.

8

Snow leopards have fur between their toes to help protect their feet from the cold snow.

When a blizzard fills the air with whirling snow, snow leopards stay in their **dens.** They wrap their long tails over their backs and heads. Their tails act like cosy scarves, keeping their ears and noses warm.

9

Size, shape and speed

Snow leopards are large and powerful.
When fully grown, they measure up to 1.5
metres long from their noses to the tips of their
tails – that's twice the length of a pet cat.
Males are larger than females.
Really big males can weigh up to
70 kilograms – that's as much
as 14 pet cats.

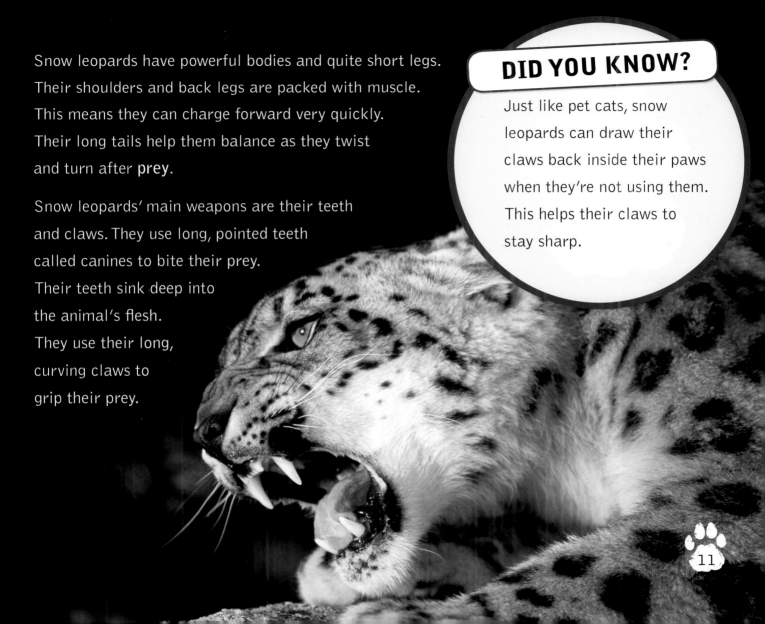

Snow leopards have powerful bodies and quite short legs. Their shoulders and back legs are packed with muscle. This means they can charge forward very quickly. Their long tails help them balance as they twist and turn after **prey**.

Snow leopards' main weapons are their teeth and claws. They use long, pointed teeth called canines to bite their prey. Their teeth sink deep into the animal's flesh. They use their long, curving claws to grip their prey.

DID YOU KNOW?

Just like pet cats, snow leopards can draw their claws back inside their paws when they're not using them. This helps their claws to stay sharp.

11

Keep out!

Each snow leopard has its own hunting ground, called a territory. Snow leopards regularly visit the borders of their territory and spray the rocks there with urine. The smelly urine acts as a signal, telling other snow leopards that this patch of land is taken. Keep out or there'll be trouble! If one leopard finds another on its patch, it will snarl ferociously and drive the stranger out.

In areas where there is plenty of food, the territory for a single snow leopard can be quite small — about 40 square kilometres, which is the size of 4,000 football pitches. Where there is less food, each leopard needs a hunting area up to five times this size.

What do snow leopards eat?

Like all cats, snow leopards hunt other animals for food. They like to eat sheep and goats, but the adult animals are quick and **sure-footed**. Snow leopards go after lambs and **kids** because the young animals are easier to catch. Snow leopards that do manage to catch an adult goat will not need to hunt again for two weeks. In a year, adult snow leopards may eat up to 30 goats or sheep.

a wild markhor goat

DID YOU KNOW?

Snow leopards have been known to kill animals that are three times their own weight.

Snow leopards also hunt animals as big as deer and as fierce as boars. If food is **scarce**, they will go after smaller prey such as hares, and mountain rodents called marmots. The only mountain animals that snow leopards don't hunt are huge, hairy cattle called yaks – they're just too large and fierce, and have sharp horns.

a marmot

Keen senses

Snow leopards mostly hunt at dusk and dawn when it is almost dark. Their **senses** help them to find food in very dim light. They can see well even if it is almost completely dark. Their long, sensitive whiskers help them feel their way at night.

Snow leopards have very good senses of smell and hearing. They can hear the tiny rustle of a marmot moving through the grass. Snow leopards' keen noses can identify hundreds of different smells. They can sniff a faint trace of scent and are able to tell whether a goat, sheep, marmot or human has passed by days ago. If another snow leopard has left its scent, they can tell whether the animal was male or female and whether it was young or old.

Snow leopards cock their ears to catch faint sounds made by prey.

Stalking and ambushing

Snow leopards hunt alone. They do this by stalking their prey.
When they spy a sheep or a goat, they crouch close to the ground,
and hide behind rocks as they creep closer and closer.
The leopards' spotted coats help them to hide among
rocks or in the shadowy forest. When leopards
are near enough, they charge forward
and leap on their prey. They bite behind
the animal's head, which
breaks its neck.

Snow leopards also lie in wait and **ambush** their prey. They settle on a rocky **crag** and sit for hours without moving a muscle. Sheep or goats that don't know the leopard is there slowly move closer. Snow leopards are very patient. Finally, when a prey animal comes into range, they drop on to it from above.

Having cubs

Snow leopards usually live alone.
The only time you see two adult
snow leopards together is when
the females are ready to mate.
This happens in late winter.
After mating, male snow
leopards return to their
own territories.

Fourteen weeks after mating, the female gives birth in a cave in the rocks. Two or three cubs are born, in a group called a litter. Newborn snow leopard cubs are tiny. They only weigh about 500 grams – that's not much heavier than a kitten. Their eyes are tightly closed, so they cannot see. They snuggle into their mother's soft fur and drink her milk.

DID YOU KNOW?

Female snow leopards line their dens with fur pulled from their own coats to make cosy nests for their cubs.

Growing up

After about a week, the cubs' eyes open. They start to crawl around and explore the den. By five weeks old, they're walking and scrambling over their mother. At two months old, they start to eat meat, which their mother brings back to the den.

Not long after this, the cubs leave the den for the first time, and start to explore the world outside. They go with their mother when she goes hunting. They learn to keep very quiet while she waits in ambush. They try to copy what she does, pouncing on small creatures such as mice and insects. As their hunting skills improve, they catch their first prey.

At about two years old, the cubs are ready to leave home. They set out to find hunting grounds of their own.

Snow leopards in danger

Snow leopards are very rare. Over the last 200 years, hunters have killed many leopards for their fur, which is used to make warm coats. Hunters also kill animals such as marmots that the snow leopards eat, either for meat or for their fur. When food becomes difficult to find in the wild, hungry snow leopards will kill sheep and goats on farms. This gets them into trouble with farmers, who will shoot them if they can.

Snow leopards are now so rare that they're in danger of dying out altogether. There may only be about 5,000 of these big cats left in the wild. No one is certain how many there are, however, because snow leopards are so good at hiding. About 400 more snow leopards live in zoos.

Snow leopards cannot protect themselves against humans shooting at them.

Breeding snow leopards in zoos helps to keep the population up.

Saving snow leopards

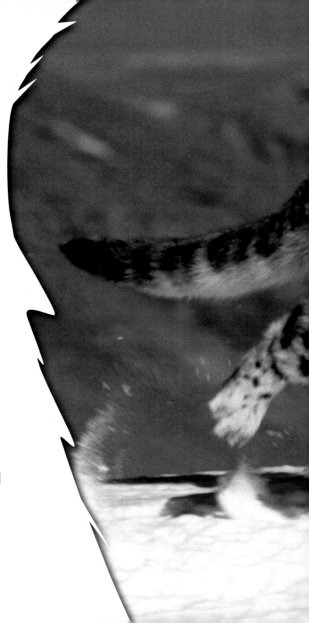

People are now trying to protect snow leopards.
In countries where snow leopards live, it is now against
the law to hunt them. However, people called **poachers**
carry on hunting. They're willing to run the risk of being
caught because snow leopard fur is very valuable.
A poacher can earn a lot of money selling just one
dead leopard.

Many of the wild places where snow leopards live
have now been made into protected areas, such as
national parks. This saves the leopards from poachers,
but also protects all the animals that they eat, and
their surroundings. It is important that everyone knows
how rare snow leopards are. The more that we can find
out about them, the more snow leopards can be protected
in the wild.

Glossary

ambush	a surprise attack
crag	a steep cliff
dens	the hidden homes of wild animals
kids	young goats
national parks	areas of land or water that are protected by the government
poachers	people who hunt and catch wildlife on land that is not their own
prey	an animal that is hunted and eaten by other animals
scarce	when there is not very much of something
senses	what a living thing uses to help it to get information about its surroundings, such as sight, smell, hearing, taste and touch
sure-footed	unlikely to fall or slip

Index

Snow leopards

Tails are used for balance while chasing after prey, and to keep the leopards warm.

Strong back legs allow leopards to leap long distances to catch prey.

Furry coats grow extra-thick in winter to help keep them warm.

Paws with rubbery soles help leopards to grip rock and ice.

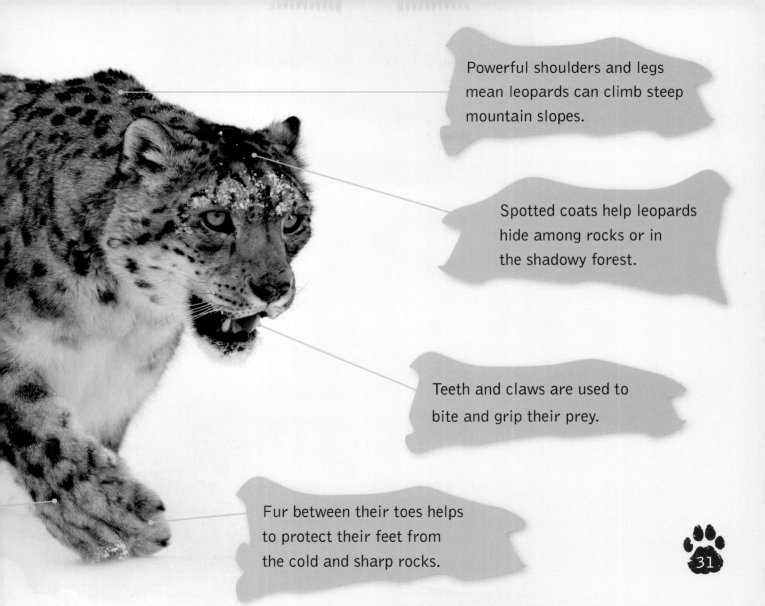

Powerful shoulders and legs mean leopards can climb steep mountain slopes.

Spotted coats help leopards hide among rocks or in the shadowy forest.

Teeth and claws are used to bite and grip their prey.

Fur between their toes helps to protect their feet from the cold and sharp rocks.

Ideas for reading

Written by Gillian Howell
Primary Literacy Consultant

Learning objectives: *(word reading objectives correspond with Lime band; all other objectives correspond with Copper band)* read aloud books closely matched to their improving phonic knowledge, sounding out unfamiliar words accurately, automatically and without undue hesitation; reading books that are structured in different ways and reading for a range of purposes; identifying main ideas drawn from more than one paragraph and summarising these; retrieve and record information from non-fiction

Curriculum links: Geography

Interest words: disguise, camouflage, cheetahs, jaguars, whirling, urine, ferociously, stalking, patient

Word count: 1,790

Resources: pens, paper, internet, art materials

Getting started

- Read the title together and look at the front cover. Ask the children what they can see and what they think the book is about. Ask them what they know about snow leopards.

- Turn to the back cover and read the blurb together, then ask the children to read the contents page aloud. Ask them if they think it will make any difference to the information if they read chapters in sequence or dip in to particular chapters that interest them first.

Reading and responding

- Turn to p2 and find the word *disguise*. If any children have difficulty reading it, ask them to break it into chunks. Explain that the *u* is silent as in *guide*. Discuss other strategies they could use when they meet unfamiliar words.

- Ask the children to read the text aloud but in a quiet voice. Ask them to make notes as they read of key points that affect snow leopards. Listen in to the children and prompt as necessary, ensuring they have an understanding of what they're reading.

- On p18, pause and ask the children to explain what stalking is and find where the word is explained in the text.